HEALTHY AND HAPPY

Harmful Substances

Louise Spilsbury

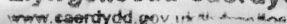

Published in 2013 by Wayland
Copyright © Wayland 2013

Wayland, 338 Euston Road, London NW1 3BH
Wayland, Level 17/207 Kent Street, Sydney, NSW 2000

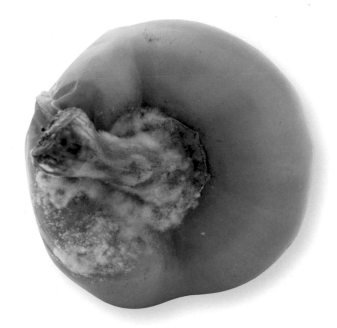

British Library Cataloguing in Publication Data
Spilsbury, Louise.
   Harmful substances. — (Healthy and happy)
   1. Substance abuse—Juvenile literature.
   I. Title II. Series
   613.8-dc22

ISBN 978-0-7502-7174-5

Produced for Wayland by Calcium
Design: Paul Myerscough and Geoff Ward
Editor: Sarah Eason
Editor for Wayland: Joyce Bentley
Illustrations: Geoff Ward
Picture research: Maria Joannou
Consultant: Sue Beck, MSc, BSc

Printed in China

Pic credits: Corbis: Georgi Licovksi/EPA 22; Fotolia: Lucky Dragon 2, 8; Getty Images: Iconica 20, Riser/Barry Austin Photography 6; Istockphoto: Gary Alvis 11, Perkmeup Imagery 27, Princessdlaf 21; Shutterstock: 9, Galina Barskaya 25, Andrey Bayda 7, DNF-Style Photography 18, Gelpi 23, Jack Hollingsworth 26, Kameel4u 4, Sergey Lavrentev 12, Monkey Business Images 5, Varina and Jay Patel 14, Rosy Black 16, Julián Rovagnati 19, Sianc 15, Audrey Snider-Bell 13, Fred Sweet 10, Tomasz Trojanowski 1, Shane White 17, Vladimir Wrangel 24.

Cover photograph: Shutterstock/Gelpi

Wayland is a division of Hachette Children's Books, an Hachette UK company.

www.hachette.co.uk

Contents

A happy, healthy body

To look after your body, you need to know which substances are safe and which are harmful. Harmful substances can damage your body and stop it from working.

It's a fact!

Every year around 30,000 children are **poisoned** by harmful substances.

Your body is more amazing than any machine. Look after it!

A healthy body

Your body is made up of different parts such as the skin, **heart** and brain. They work together to keep you healthy. If a harmful substance damages one part, your whole body may not work properly.

Growing up safely

Children have smaller bodies than adults. That is why harmful substances are more dangerous for children. Knowing how to take care of your body will keep you safe.

Keeping healthy can help you and your friends to feel happier.

5

Around the house

Many substances we use around the house are helpful. These include cleaning products, toiletries and air sprays. These products make life easier when they are used properly.

Chemical danger

Many cleaning products are harmful if they get onto your skin or into your body. Household cleaners contain strong **chemicals**. Bleach and disinfectant can burn your skin. If you swallow them, they can burn your mouth, throat or stomach. Others can even kill you.

Leave cleaning with harmful products to adults, such as your parents or carers.

Read the labels

Most household substances have labels that tell people how to use them. The labels also tell people if the substances are dangerous. People should check the labels carefully.

A skull and crossbones sign warns you that a substance could kill you or hurt you very badly.

It's a fact!

Children should never touch substances that can be harmful. They should be used by adults only.

In the kitchen

People store and prepare food in the kitchen. We need to eat food to be healthy, but sometimes it can be harmful.

Food poisoning

Food poisoning can make you very ill. It is caused by eating rotten food, or food that has not been cooked properly. Keep food in the fridge to stop it going rotten.

Food poisoning

Wash your hands when you prepare or eat food. **Germs** on dirty hands can also make you sick.

Rotten food, such as this pepper, may have mould on it. Never eat rotten food – it can make you very ill.

Boiling water

Boiling water is so hot that it can burn your skin. Take care near kettles and pans on the hob. You could knock boiling liquids over yourself.

It's a fact!

'E numbers' are substances used in food. Some can change the way you feel. They can be found in foods such as sweets.

Some E numbers can make you angry or upset. Try to avoid foods that contain them.

In the bathroom

Many substances in the bathroom come in beautiful bottles and smell good. They may look tempting, but they can be harmful.

Being curious

When something looks and smells good, you might feel like tasting it. Bathroom products such as bubble baths have fruity smells, but you should never taste them. They contain chemicals that can make you sick.

Don't try on make-up. It may contain chemicals that could harm your skin.

Mixing substances

Some substances are dangerous when they are mixed together. Mixing bleach and toilet cleaners create dangerous **fumes**. They can choke or poison you if you breathe them in.

HEALTHY HINTS

Bottles without a label may contain harmful substances. Do not touch them.

Ask your parents or carers to put harmful substances out of reach of younger brothers and sisters.

Pets

Pets are fun to have around and they can help us feel happy. However, they can also make substances that may harm you.

Keeping clean

Cat and dog faeces (poo) contain substances that can make you very ill. Animals clean themselves by licking their bodies, including their bottoms. Tiny amounts of faeces can be all over an animal's body. You should always wash your hands after touching pets.

If a pet licks your face or hands, wash yourself straight away.

It's a fact!

The hairs from a tarantula's legs are dangerous. If they get into your eyes, they can cause blindness.

Some people keep exotic pets, such as tarantulas.

Allergies

An **allergy** is when someone becomes ill because of a substance that may be harmless to other people. When cats lick their bodies, their saliva (spit) dries and floats into the air. If people with allergies breathe in the dried spit, their eyes and nose become red, itchy and sore, and they sneeze.

In the garden

Playing outside is great fun and keeps you healthy. But there are some harmful substances to watch out for in the garden.

Substances in the soil

There are trillions of germs in every spoonful of soil! They can make you sick or give you **diarrhoea**. Germs get into your body when you put dirty fingers near your mouth or eyes. Wash your hands after playing outside.

It is best to wear garden gloves when you are digging in soil.

HEALTHY HINTS

Some garden products can burn your skin and poison you if you touch or swallow them. Wash your hands and tell an adult if you ever touch them by mistake.

Always ask an adult before eating or touching any plants.

Plant poisons

Some plants are good to eat, but some can harm you. Colourful berries may look tasty, but they could be poisonous. Some plants make a juice called **sap** that can burn or blister your skin if you touch it.

In the garage

Besides cars and bikes, there may be substances in the garage. These could include paint, petrol and garden sprays. Some of them can be harmful.

Harmful effects

Different substances have different effects. If you touch car wax, for example, your skin may become sore. Other chemicals are more dangerous. Drinking just a small amount of **antifreeze** can kill you.

Only adults should use the substances kept in a garage.

16

Fire hazards

Many substances found in the garage are flammable. This means that they catch fire easily. Petrol and paint cleaners are highly flammable. If you touch or move the bottles that contain these substances, they might spill out and catch fire. It is best not to touch them at all.

It's a fact!

Flammable substances come in bottles or tins with a fire symbol on them.

A fire symbol on a bottle tells you that the substance inside it is flammable.

What are drugs?

Different drugs do different things to the body. Drugs called medicines make people feel better when they ill. Other drugs, such as caffeine, can harm the body.

You will sleep better if you avoid drinks that contain caffeine.

What is caffeine?

Caffeine is a drug found in coffee, tea and some fizzy drinks. In small amounts, caffeine is harmless. A lot of caffeine can give you headaches and stop you sleeping. It can also give some people chest pains. Caffeine affects children more than adults because their bodies are smaller. Most schools do not allow caffeine drinks in their canteens.

It's a fact!

Caffeine is found in over 60 plants around the world.

Avoid drinks that contain caffeine, such as cola. Milk, water and fruit juice are better choices.

Taking medicines

Most people take medicines occasionally, when they feel ill. Other people have long-lasting illnesses and they need to take medicine every day.

Rules about medicines

Medicines become harmful substances if you take them when you do not need them or if you take too much. You should only take medicine that a doctor has given you. Always ask an adult to give you the medicine.

A parent or carer is the best person to give you the medicine you need.

Vitamins and minerals

Some people take **vitamins** and **minerals** to stay healthy. For example, some adults take iron tablets to keep their blood healthy. An **overdose** of iron tablets is very dangerous for children.

HEALTHY HINTS

Never eat a sweet that you find lying around. Some medicines look like sweets and could harm you if you swallow them.

If you take vitamins, make sure you take the right amount.

21

Harmful gases

Substances such as glue and petrol give off fumes. Some people breathe the fumes to feel dizzy and giggly. Sniffing harmful substances is very dangerous.

It's a fact!

If a person sniffs a substance such as glue, it can stop their heart beating and kill them.

Never let your friends force you into sniffing substances. It could kill you.

What happens?

Sniffing chemicals quickly makes you feel out of control. You can see things that are not really there, which can be very scary. Worst of all, the fumes can damage important body parts, such as your brain, eyes and **lungs**. You could even die.

How to say 'no'

Some people sniff substances because their friends do it and want them to try it, too. It is better to say 'no' and not be friends with someone than to hurt yourself.

Say 'no' clearly and firmly. Walk away if necessary.

Cigarettes and alcohol

Friends always encourage you to try new things. But if a friend suggests you try cigarettes or alcohol, the only answer to give them is 'no'!

Cigarettes

Cigarettes contain substances that damage your lungs. They cause a disease called lung cancer, which can kill. Cigarettes also make clothes and hair smell. They can turn teeth yellow and cause bad breath, a nasty cough and dry, wrinkly skin!

Stay away from people who smoke – the smoke can damage your lungs.

Alcohol

Adults can drink alcohol, but children should avoid it. Even a tiny bit of alcohol is dangerous when you are young. It slows down your brain and makes you do things that you wouldn't normally do. Drinking too much alcohol too quickly can even kill.

People who do not smoke can enjoy sports and keeping fit.

Who can help?

If you want to find out more about harmful substances, there are some things you can do. By knowing more, you can help to keep yourself and others safe.

People to ask

Always ask an adult who you can trust if you are not sure whether something is safe or dangerous. This could be someone in your family, such as a grandparent, parent or carer. You could also talk to a teacher, youth club worker or police officer.

When you ring a doctor or NHS Direct for help, stay calm and tell them what is wrong.

In an emergency

Get help straight away if you or someone you know has swallowed, touched or breathed in a harmful substance. Call NHS Direct on 0845 4647 or dial the emergency services on 999. Take the bottle or packet the substance was in with you if you go to the doctor or to hospital.

HEALTHY HINTS

Never touch anything unless you have asked an adult if it is safe.

Knowing how to stay safe can help you to help others if they need it.

Make a board game

You will need:

- square piece of cardboard
- colouring pencils
- milk bottle tops
- dice

Make this special version of Snakes & Ladders and teach your friends about harmful substances.

1. Divide your cardboard into 49 squares – seven rows of seven squares. Mark the square at the bottom left 'Start' and the square at the top right 'Finish'.

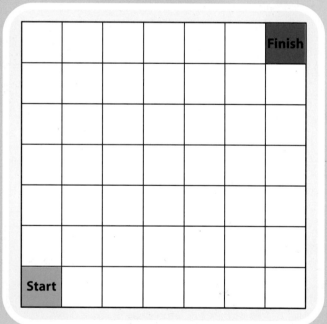

						Finish
Start						

43	44	45	46	47	48	Finish 49
42	41	40	39	38	37	36
29	30	31	32	33	34	35
28	27	26	25	24	23	22
15	16	17	18	19	20	21
14	13	12	11	10	9	8
Start 1	2	3	4	5	6	7

2. Number all the squares. The first row should go left to right, the second row right to left, the third row left to right, and so on.

3. On 6 squares, draw a skull and crossbones with a snake slithering from the square to another square (see right). These are harmful squares. You can also add other harmful squares with lightning and fire symbols (see below). If you land on any harmful squares, slide down the snake or go back a square.

4. Add some harmless squares with a ladder (see above). If you land on these, climb up the ladder. Use crosses, ticks and arrows to decorate the rest of the squares.

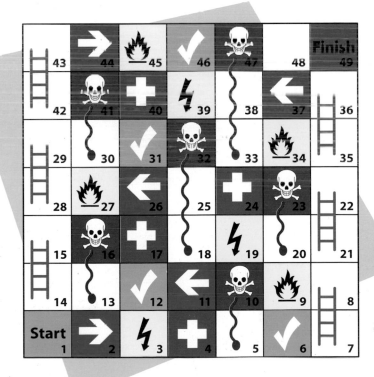

5. Use coloured bottle tops for counters to play the game.

Harmful substances topic web

Use this topic web to discover themes and ideas in subjects that are related to harmful substances.

HARMFUL SUBSTANCES

PSHE

- How to recognise warning symbols.
- Understanding that some substances can be harmful.
- What to do if you come into contact with a harmful substance.
- How to help others in an emergency situation.
- Who to turn to for help in the event of an emergency.
- Taking responsibility for personal safety and safety of others.
- Write a list of the things in your house that contain harmful substances.

SCIENCE

- How the body works and why some substances can harm it.
- Understanding that substances can contain harmful chemicals.
- Understanding that caffeine, alcohol and cigarettes are harmful substances.
- Why medicines and vitamins may be harmful.
- Write a plan about what do to if you touch or swallow a harmful substance.

ART AND DESIGN

- How to design and make a board game about harmful substances from cardboard, pens and bottle tops.

Glossary

allergy when someone's body reacts badly to substances that are normally harmless to other people

antifreeze chemical added to a car radiator to stop it from freezing

chemicals substances that affect how the body behaves

diarrhoea illness that gives people runny poo

fumes smoke or gas that smells or may be dangerous if breathed in

germs tiny living things. Some germs are useful; others cause disease

heart a muscular organ that pumps blood around the body

lungs organs in the chest that people use to breathe

minerals substances in the earth, such as iron or salt

overdose when someone takes too much of a drug at one time

poisoned when someone is made very ill by a harmful substance

sap liquid that carries food through plants

vitamins essential substances found in food that people need to stay healthy

Find out more

Books

Health Choices: Harmful Substances by Cath Senker (Wayland, 2007)

Keeping Healthy: Harmful Substances by Carol Ballard (Wayland, 2008)

Websites

Find out more about smoking at the Kids Against Tobacco Smoke website:
http://kats.roycastle.org/

Join two secret agents investigating toxic substances at:
http://re-solv.org/toxic_agents/index.htm

Index